RENAL DIET COOKBOOK FOR BEGINNERS

The bible of healthy kidneys. Low sodium, low potassium & Low-Phosphorus delicious and easy-to-cook recipes. FULL COLOR EDITION

Margaret Salt

Introduction

Kidney disease is a widespread condition that affects roughly 10% of the world's population

The kidneys are little but mighty bean-shaped organs that are involved in a variety of vital activities. They are in charge of filtering waste, releasing hormones to regulate blood pressure, regulating fluids in the body, generating urine, and a variety of other vital functions

There are several ways in which these important organs can be harmed.

The most frequent risk factors for renal disease are high blood pressure and diabetes. smoking, Obesity, genetics, age and, gender, on the other hand, can all enhance the risk

uncontrolled blood sugar and High blood pressure damage blood vessels in the kidneys, limiting their ability to function optimally

When the kidneys fail to function effectively, waste accumulates in the blood, especially waste products from the diet

As a result, persons with the renal illness must adhere to a particular diet known as renal diet.

Table of content

Introduction

Kidney disease is a widespread condition that affects roughly 10% of the world's population

The kidneys are little but mighty bean-shaped organs that are involved in a variety of vital activities. They are in charge of filtering waste, releasing hormones to regulate blood pressure, regulating fluids in the body, generating urine, and a variety of other vital functions

There are several ways in which these important organs can be harmed.

The most frequent risk factors for renal disease are high blood pressure and diabetes. smoking, Obesity, genetics, age and, gender, on the other hand, can all enhance the risk

uncontrolled blood sugar and High blood pressure damage blood vessels in the kidneys, limiting their ability to function optimally

When the kidneys fail to function effectively, waste accumulates in the blood, especially waste products from the diet

As a result, persons with the renal illness must adhere to a particular diet known as renal diet.

Chapter 1 What Is Renal Diet

A kidney diet is low in salt, phosphorus, and protein. A renal diet also emphasizes the significance of eating high-quality protein and, in most cases, minimizing fluids. Some people may additionally require potassium and calcium restrictions. Because each person's body is unique, each patient must collaborate with a renal dietitian to develop a diet that is matched to the patient's needs.

The following are some substances that must be monitored in order to support a renal diet:

1.1. Sodium And Its Role in The Body

Sodium is a mineral that may be found in various natural foods. Most people consider salt and sodium to be interchangeable. Salt, on the other hand, is a sodium chloride substance. Foods that we consume may include salt or sodium in various ways. Because of the additional salt, processed foods frequently have greater sodium levels.

Sodium is one of the three primary electrolytes in the body (chloride and potassium are the other two). Electrolytes regulate the flow of fluids into and out of the body's tissues and cells. Sodium is involved in:

- Controlling blood pressure and volume
- Balancing how much fluid the body retains or excretes
- Nerve function and muscle contraction are regulated.
- Keeping the blood's acid-base balance in check

Keeping Track of Salt Intake

Excess sodium and fluid from the body can be hazardous for patients with renal disease because their kidneys cannot efficiently clear excess salt and fluid. As salt and fluid accumulate in the tissues and circulation, they may result in:

- heightened thirst
- Edema is defined as swelling in the legs, hands, and face.
- Blood pressure is too high.
- Excess fluid in the circulation can overwork your heart, causing it to expand and weaken.
- Shortness of breath: fluid can accumulate in the lungs, making breathing harder.

Ways To Keep Track of Salt Intake

- Read food labels at all times. The amount of sodium in a product is always mentioned.
- Take note of the serving sizes.
- Fresh meats should be used instead than processed meats
- Choose fresh fruits and vegetables or canned and frozen products with no added salt.
- Avoid eating processed meals.
- Compare brands and choose goods with the lowest sodium content.
- Use spices that do not have "salt" in their name (choose garlic powder to replace garlic salt.)
- Cook at home without using salt.

- The total salt level should be kept at 400 mg each meal and 150 mg every snack.

1.2. Potassium And Its Role in The Body

Potassium is a mineral that may be found in many foods and naturally in the body. Potassium helps keep the heartbeat normal, and the muscles operate properly. Potassium is also required for fluid and electrolyte balance in the bloodstream. The kidneys assist in maintaining a healthy level of potassium in the body by excreting excess quantities in the urine.

Keeping A Close Eye on Potassium Intake

When the kidneys fail, they can no longer eliminate extra potassium from the body, causing potassium levels to rise. Hyperkalemia is a condition in which there is an excess of potassium in the blood, which can result in:

- Muscle deterioration
- An erratic heartbeat
- The pulse is slow.
- Attacks on the heart
- Death

Ways to Keep Track of Potassium Intake

When the kidneys no longer control potassium, a patient must track how much potassium enters the body.

To help keep your potassium levels in check, try the following changes:

- Consult a renal dietician about developing an eating plan.
- Choose fruits and vegetables that are in season.
- Limit your consumption of milk and dairy products to 8 oz each day.
- Avoid potassium-containing salt alternatives and spices.
- Take note of the serving size.
- Potassium-rich foods should be avoided.
- Read the labels on packaged goods and stay away from potassium chloride.
- Keep a dietary diary.

1.3. Phosphorus And Its Role in The Body

Phosphorus is a mineral that is essential for bone formation and maintenance. Phosphorus also contributes to the growth of connective tissue and organs and the movement of muscles. When phosphorus-containing food is taken and digested, the phosphorus is absorbed by the small intestines and deposited in the bones.

Why should renal patients keep track of their Phosphorus intake?

Normal functioning kidneys may remove extra phosphorus in your blood. When kidney function is impaired, the kidneys cannot eliminate excess phosphorus. Phosphorus levels that are too high might cause calcium to be drawn out of your bones, weakening them. This also causes hazardous calcium deposits in blood vessels, lungs, eyes, and the heart.

Keeping Track of Phosphorus Consumption

Phosphorus may be present in a variety of foods. As a result, individuals with impaired kidney function should consult with a renal dietician to regulate their phosphorus levels.

Tips for keeping phosphorus levels safe:

- Learn which foods are low in phosphorus.
- Consult your doctor about using phosphate binders at mealtime.
- At meals and snacks, eat smaller servings of protein-rich foods.
- Keep a tight eye on the serving size.
- Avoid packaged foods with added phosphorus. On ingredient labels, look for phosphorus or terms beginning with "PHOS."
- Consume plenty of fresh fruits and vegetables.
- Keep a dietary diary.

1.4. Protein

Protein is not a concern for kidneys that are in good condition. Normally, protein is consumed, and waste products are produced, which are then filtered by the kidney's nephrons. The waste is then converted into the urine with the aid of extrarenal proteins. On the other hand, damaged kidneys fail to eliminate protein waste, allowing it to build in the blood.

Protein consumption might be difficult for chronic kidney disease patients since the amount varies depending on the stage of the disease. Protein is required for tissue maintenance and other body functions. Thus, it is critical to consume the quantity prescribed by your nephrologist or renal dietitian for your specific stage of illness.

1.5. Fluids

Fluid regulation is critical for patients in the latter stages of chronic kidney disease since normal fluid consumption can result in fluid buildup in the body, which can be harmful. Because dialysis patients frequently have reduced urine production, an increase in fluid in the body might place undue strain on the heart and lungs.

The fluid allotment for each patient is computed individually based on urine output and dialysis parameters. It is critical to adhere to your nephrologist's/fluid nutritionist's intake recommendations.

To keep fluid consumption under control, patients should:

- Keep an eye on the number of fluids utilized while cooking.
- Count all foods that melt at room temperature (popsicles, Jell-o, and so on).

Do not consume more than your doctor has prescribed

ictness of your food plan should be determined by your stage of renal disease. You may have few or rictions on what you eat and drink in the early stages of renal disease. As your kidney condition s, your doctor may advise you to limit:

orus

um

Chapter 2 Why Should You Follow This Diet?

Once you have chronic kidney disease, you must follow a kidney-friendly diet (CKD). Keeping a close eye on what you eat, and drink will help you stay healthy. This section contains information for persons who have a renal disease but are not on dialysis.

This data is intended to serve as a reference g. Everyone is unique, and everyone has distinct nutritional requirements. To establish a meal plan that works for you, consult a renal dietitian (a person who specializes in food and nutrition for persons with kidney disease).

Request that your doctor assists you in locating a dietician. Appointments with dietitians are covered by Medicare and much private insurance coverage. Check with your insurance provider to determine if medical nutrition treatment is covered under your coverage (MNT).

2.1. Basics of a Healthy Diet

With any meal plan, including the kidney-friendly diet, you must keep note of how much of each nutrient you consume, such as:

Calories

Protein

Fat

Carbohydrates

To ensure that you are getting enough essential nutrients, you must eat and drink in the appropriate quantity quantities. The "Nutrition Facts" label contains all of the details you need to keep a record of your consumption.

Read more about everything that is in the foods you consume by reading the nutrition data section on food labels. Each portion of a food's nutrition data will tell you how much protein, carbs, fat, and salt it contains. This can assist you in selecting meals that are high in the nutrients you require while being low in the ones you should avoid.

When looking at nutrition data, there are a few essential aspects that will provide you with the knowledge you require:

Calories

The calories you consume provide energy to your body. Calories are obtained from protein, carbs, and fat in your diet. The number of calories you require is determined by your age, gender, body size, and amount of exercise.

You would also need to change your calorie intake based on your weight-loss objectives. Some people will have to reduce their calorie intake. Others may require more calories. Your doctor or a nutritionist can advise you on how many calories you should consume each day. Work with your dietician to create a food plan that ensures you get enough calories and stay in touch for advice.

Protein

Proteins are one of your body's building components. Protein is required by your body to develop, heal, and maintain health. Protein deficiency can lead to brittle skin, hair, and nails. However, eating too much protein might be harmful. You may need to alter your protein intake to be healthy and feel your best.

The quantity of protein you should consume is determined by your body size, degree of exercise, and health issues. Some doctors advise persons with renal illness to decrease their protein intake or modify their protein source. This is because a high-protein diet causes the kidneys to work harder, perhaps causing additional damage. Ask your doctor or a nutritionist how much protein you should consume and what the best protein sources are for you.

Use the table below to determine which foods are high in protein and which are low in protein. It is important to remember that just because a food is low in protein does not mean you should consume it in large quantities.

Low-protein foods include:

- Fruits
- Bread
- Vegetables
- pasta and Rice

Protein-rich foods:

- Eggs
- Red Meat
- Fish
- Poultry

Carbohydrates

Carbohydrates ("carbs") are the simplest type of energy for your body to utilize. Vegetables and fruits are good sources of carbs. Sugar, hard candies, honey, soft drinks, and other sugary liquids are all unhealthy sources of carbs

Some carbs include a lot of phosphorus and potassium, which you should avoid depending on your stage of renal disease. We will go through this in further detail later. If you have diabetes, you may also need to keep a close eye on your carbohydrate intake. Your dietician can teach you more about the carbohydrates in your diet and how they affect your blood sugar levels.

Fat

To be healthy, you must include some fat in your diet. Fat provides energy and aids in the use of several vitamins found in meals. However, eating too much fat might result in heart disease and weight gain. Try to keep fat to a minimum in your diet plan and use healthier fats when possible.

Unsaturated fat is a healthier or "healthy" fat. Unsaturated fat examples include:

- Corn oil
- Extra virgin olive oil
- Peanuts oil

Unsaturated fat can aid in cholesterol reduction. Eat extra unsaturated fat if you need to are trying to reduce weight, keep unsaturated fat to a minimum in your diet. As is moderation is the key. Too much "healthy" fat can sometimes be harmful.

Saturated fat, generally known as "bad" fat, raises cholesterol and increases the risk Saturated fats include the following:

- Butter
- Shortening
- Lard

Meats

In your food plan, keep these to a minimum. Instead, choose unsaturated fat, which Trimming the fat from meat and removing the skin from chicken or turkey can also saturated fat. Trans fat should also be avoided. This kind of fat raises your "bad" (LDI decreasing your "good" (HDL) cholesterol. This increases your risk of developing heart lead to kidney impairment.

Portions:

Choosing nutritious meals is a good place to start, but eating too much of anything, inclu may be detrimental. Another component of a healthy diet is portion management or cor you consume.

To assist you to keep your portions under control, try the following:

Check the nutrition facts label on food to find out how much of each nutrient is in or much of each nutrient is in one serving. Many products contain multiple servings. A 2 for example, is actually two-and-a-half servings. Many fresh goods, such as vegetable have nutritional information labels. Request a list of nutrition data for fresh foods fro well as for instructions on how to measure the proper quantities.

Eat gently and quit when you are no longer hungry. It takes around 20 min fo communicate to your brain that you are full. If you eat too rapidly, you may consume you require.

Eating while doing something else, such as watching TV or driving, should be avoided how much you have eaten if you are distracted.

Do not eat the food straight from the packaging. Instead, take out one portion of foo bag or box.

Portion management is an essential component of every meal plan. It is especially friendly meal plan since you may need to limit how much of certain foods and beverag

2.2. What makes a kidney-friendly diet unique?

When your kidneys do not function properly, waste and fluid accumulate in your b additional fluid can affect bone, heart, and other health complications over time. A friendly restricts the number of specific minerals and fluids you consume. This can he moisture from accumulating and causing difficulties.

Chapter 3 Food to Eat & Avoid

The following are just a few examples of meals that individuals with diabetes and chronic kidney disease can consume. Your nutritionist can make additional recommendations and assist you in locating recipes for delectable meals:

3.1. Foods To Eat

• Fruits: grapes, berries, cherries, plums, apples,

• Veggies: onions, cauliflower, turnips, eggplant, garlic

• Proteins: lean meats (poultry, fish), egg whites, unsalted seafood, sea bass

• Carbs: white bread, sandwich buns, bagels, whole wheat pasta, unsalted crackers,

• Drinks: water, unsweetened tea, clear diet sodas,

3.2. Foods To Limit or Avoid

Here are a few lists of food items to avoid or limit according to your kidney disease:

Some High Sodium Foods to avoid

- Pancake or baking mixes
- Bread, crackers, and cereals, (some)
- Canned vegetables (rinse well, or try frozen instead)
- Canned stews and soups
- Condiments, like ketchup, soy sauce, mustard, and salad dressings
- Cottage cheese and some other cheeses
- Pretzels, chips, cheese puffs
- Foods with seasoning packets (like mac and cheese, ramen noodles, flavored rice, or pasta side dishes) and "helper" foods
- Olives and pickled foods,
- Spaghetti sauce, tomato sauce and vegetable juices.
- Frozen dinners
- Processed meats, like hot dogs, bacon, and deli meats

Some High Potassium Foods That You Must Limit

- Avocados
- Beets and beet greens
- Bananas
- Clams
- Carrot juice

- Fish (e.g., clams, halibut, cod, salmon, tuna trout)
- Dried beans, chickpeas, peas, lentils, and soybeans, (all kinds)
- "enriched" fresh meats (read tags and look for potassium content)
- Dried fruit (e.g., dates, apricots, raisins, figs, prunes — and juices)
- Jerusalem artichokes
- Hard squash (e.g., butternut acorn)
- Milk (non–fat)
- Mangos
- Molasses
- Melons, like cantaloupe
- Nuts
- Parsnips
- Oranges
- Salt substitutes
- Spinach
- Sweet potatoes and potatoes
- Tomato products and tomatoes
- Low-fat yogurt

Sweets and Starches (You May Want to Limit)

- Candy
- Corn and corn products (chips, cereal, puffs, etc.)
- Hard squash
- Plantains
- Ice cream
- Potatoes and sweet potatoes
- Peas, dried beans, lentils, etc. (too high in potassium)
- Wheat products (bread, bagels, cereal, cake, crackers, muffins, etc.)
- Rice cereal (and white rice)

3.3. Tips For Healthy Kidneys

Here are some suggestions to help you maintain a healthy kidney.

• Maintain an active and healthy lifestyle.

• Maintain a healthy blood sugar level.

• Keep an eye on your blood pressure.

- Maintain a healthy weight and consume a balanced diet.

- Maintain an adequate hydration intake.

- Avoid smoking.

- Keep track of the number of OTC (over the counter) medications you use.

- If you are at high risk, get your kidney function evaluated.

RENAL DIET RECIPES

Microwave Coffee Cup Egg Scramble

INGREDIENTS

- **2 EGG WHITES LARGE**
- **1 EGG LARGE**
- **1/8 TSP BLACK PEPPER**
- **2 TBSP MILK1% LOW FAT**

2 MINUTES   **2 SERVINGS**

Instructions:

- Using cooking spray, coat a 12 oz coffee mug. In the mug, whisk together the egg whites, milk, and egg until smooth.

- Microwave the coffee mug for 45 sec, then remove and mix. Microwave for another 30-45 sec, or until the eggs are completely set.

- Dust with pepper and serve.
  Suggestions:
- The cooking time of microwaves varies. To avoid overdone eggs, make adjustments as needed.

- To enhance flavor, add mushrooms 1/4 cup of onion or bell pepper.

- If desired, add a dash of spicy sauce.

Nutritional Values: Calories 117kcal | Protein 15g | Fat 5g | Carbs 3g | Salt 194 mg |Sugar 1g |Fibers 0g

Berry Almond Oatmeal

INGREDIENTS

- 1 CUP OLD-FASHIONED OATS
- 2 CUP WATER
- 2 TBSP SLICED ALMONDS
- 1/4 TSP SALT
- 1/4 CUP FRESH OR FROZEN BLUEBERRIES
- 3 PACKET SPLENDA SWEETENER
- 1/4 TSP ALMOND EXTRACT

5 MINUTES   2 SERVINGS

Instructions:

- Put water to boil in a saucepan. Mix in the oats and salt. Cook for 5 min, stirring regularly, over medium heat.

- Add in the fruit, sweetener, almonds, and the extract into the saucepan

Suggestion:

For creamier oats, replace the water with milk (this will alter the nutrition data per serving).

Nutritional Values: Calories 220kcal | Protein 7g | Fat 7g | Carbs 33g | Salt 290mg |Sugar 4g |Fibers 5g

Apple Walnut French Toast

INGREDIENTS

- 1 TSP OLIVE OIL (OR UNSALTED BUTTER)
- 1/2 CUP EGG SUBSTITUTE
- 1/2 CUP APPLE(DICED)
- 1/2 TSP SUGAR
- 1/8 TSP NUTMEG
- 1/8 TSP (PLUS 1/4 TSP, DIVIDED) GROUND CINNAMON
- 4(ROUNDS) CLOUD BREAD
- 1TBSP MAPLE SYRUP
- 1 OZ WALNUTS

10 MINUTES 2 SERVINGS

Instructions:

- Heat a large nonstick pan to medium-high heat with 1 tbsp of butter, 1/2 tsp of cinnamon and apples; simmer, often stirring, for 5 to 7 min, or until apples soften. To keep the apples warm, place them in a shallow dish and cover them with foil. Wipe the skillet clean with a paper towel and set it aside for later.

- In a clean mixing dish, combine the egg replacement, nutmeg, sugar, and 1/2 tsp of cinnamon.

- Reheat the skillet over medium heat. Swirl in the remaining butter to coat the base.

- Put the rounds of cloud bread round into the beaten egg mixture, coating both sides. Lay the rounds in the skillet and fry for 2 to 3 min each side, or until they begin to brown.

- Distribute the rounds among the plates. If preferred, garnish with maple syrup, walnuts, apples, and a thin sprinkling of powdered sugar.

Nutritional Values: Calories 290kcal | Protein 12g | Fat 22g | Carbs 13g | Salt 280mg |Sugar 9g |Fibers 2g

Avocado Toast with Egg

INGREDIENTS

- 2 SLICES OF WHOLE-GRAIN BREAD
- 1/2 MEDIUM HASS AVOCADO
- 2 LARGE EGGS
- 1 TBSP LIME JUICE
- 1 TBSP PARSLEY
- 1/8 TSP SALT
- 1/8 TSP GROUND BLACK PEPPER
- 2 TBSP CRUMBLED FETA CHEESE

5 MINUTES   2 SERVINGS

Instructions:

- Toast the pieces of bread. Set aside the chopped parsley.

- Mash half an avocado with a fork after removing the peel. Mix in the juice of half a lime and salt. Distribute the mixture on each slice of bread.

- Heat a skillet over medium heat, sprayed with cooking spray. Cook the eggs until they are done to your liking in a skillet.

- Transfer the eggs from the skillet and place them on top of the avocado on each toast along with 1 tbsp of feta cheese, minced parsley, then ground black pepper should be sprinkled on top of each egg.

Suggestions:

Avocados contain a lot of potassium. When potassium levels are sufficiently regulated, you can still eat it on a renal diet by limiting the quantity to 1/4th of a medium avocado (around 1/4 cup). Individual advice can be obtained from your nutritionist.

Nutritional Values: Calories 225kcal | Protein | Fat 13g | Carbs 15g | Salt 404mg |Sugar 2g |Fibers 4.3 g

Fluffy Homemade Buttermilk Pancakes

INGREDIENTS

- 1/2 CUPS OF ALL-PURPOSE FLOUR
- 1/2 CUPS LOW-FAT BUTTERMILK
- 1/4 TSP CREAM OF TARTAR
- 1/2 TBSP SUGAR
- 1 TBSP CANOLA OIL AND 1 TBSP CANOLA OIL (FOR COOKING)
- 1/2 LARGE EGGS
- 1/3 TSP BAKING SODA

10 MINUTES 2 SERVINGS

Instructions:

- Preheat a skillet over medium heat

- In a large mixing bowl, combine the dry ingredients. Combine the dry ingredients with the oil, buttermilk, and egg mixture. Combine the dry ingredients with a whisk or spoon until thoroughly wet.

- Oil the skillet with a tbsp of canola oil. Spread the pancake mixture onto the skillet with a 1/3-cup measuring cup. One pancake should be around 4 inches in diameter. Allow roughly 2" between pancakes to allow for easy flipping. Turn the pancakes with a spatula when the bubbles on the top have mostly vanished. Let the other side cook until brown, and the middle is no longer damp.

- Transfer to a serving platter.

- Serve with fresh berries and a side of eggs for a healthy twist.

Nutritional Values Calories 217kcal | Protein 6g | Fat 9g | Carbs 27g | Salt 330mg |Sugar 5g |Fibers 1g

Blueberry Almond Chicken Salad Lettuce Wraps

INGREDIENTS

- 1 1/2 CUP COOKED CHICKEN (CHOPPED)
- 1/4 CUP PLAIN NONFAT GREEK YOGURT
- 1 1/2 CUP BLUEBERRIES
- 4 ICEBERG OR BIBB LETTUCE LEAVES
- 1/8 CUP FRESH BASIL (CHOPPED)
- 1/4 CUP CELERY (CHOPPED)
- 1/8 CUP GREEN ONION (OR SCALLION) (CHOPPED)
- 1/4 TSP SALT (KOSHER)
- 1/8 TSP BLACK PEPPER
- 1 TBSP ALMONDS (SLICED AND TOASTED)

10 MINUTES   2 SERVINGS

Instructions:

- In a big bowl, add yogurt, pepper salt, and basil until well combined.
- Toss in the chicken, scallions, blueberries, and celery until evenly covered.
- Place lettuce leaves on a serving dish and top with chicken mixture, distributing evenly among the lettuce leaves.
- Serve with almonds on top.

Nutritional Values: Calories 260kcal | Protein 39g | Fat 6g | Carbs 11g | Salt 350mg |Sugar 7g |Fibers 3g

Signature Skillet Supper

INGREDIENTS

- 1/3 CUP ONION(S) (CHOPPED)
- 1 TSP EXTRA VIRGIN OLIVE OIL
- 1 CLOVE GARLIC(MINCED)
- 1/3 LBS. LEAN GROUND BEEF (I USED 93% LEAN)
- FROZEN MIXED VEGETABLES1 CUP
- 1 CUP NO YOLK MEDIUM NOODLES UNCOOKED
- 1/2 CUP 1 CUP BEEF BROTH (LOW SODIUM)
- 1/2 TSP TOGARASHI (A JAPANESE PEPPER BLEND)
- WATER

30 MINUTES 2 SERVINGS

Instructions:

- In a large skillet or pan, heat the olive oil. Cook until the onions, meat, and garlic are browned. Mix in the veggies and seasonings well. Toss in the noodles gently. Pour in the broth and enough water to cover everything completely.

- Bring the water to a boil. Reduce the heat to medium and simmer until the noodles are cooked for about 15 min.

Nutritional Values: Calories 285kcal | Protein 23g | Fat 8g | Carbs28g | Salt 170mg |Sugar 5g |Fibers 6g

BBQ Chicken Pita Pizza

INGREDIENTS

- 4 OZ CHICKEN, COOKED
- 2 PITA BREAD, 6-1/2" SIZE
- 2 TBSP CRUMBLED FETA CHEESE
- 3 TBSP LOW-SODIUM BARBECUE SAUCE
- 1/8 TSP GARLIC POWDER
- 1/4 CUP PURPLE ONION

15 MINUTES   2 SERVINGS

Instructions:

- Preheat the oven to 350 degrees Fahrenheit.

- Put two pitas on a baking pan sprayed with nonstick cooking spray.

- On every pita, spread 1 1/2 tbsp BBQ sauce.

- Chop the onion and distribute it on the pitas.

- Cube the chicken and distribute it over pita bread.

- Over the pitas, sprinkle with feta cheese and garlic powder.

- Bake for between 11 and 13 min.

- Pita pizzas should be eaten immediately after baking to avoid becoming too crunchy.

Suggestions:

Read the nutrition labels and select the feta cheese and pitas with the minimum salt content.

Nutritional Values: Calories 320kcal | Protein 23g | Fat 9g | Carbs37g | Salt 523mg |Sugar 4g |Fibers 2.4g

Grilled Chicken, Asparagus & Corn

INGREDIENTS

- 2 TBSP OLIVE OIL
- 8 OZ (1 LARGE OR 2 MEDIUM BREASTS) BONELESS, SKINLESS CHICKEN BREAST
- 10 ASPARAGUS SPEARS
- 1/2 TSP CRACKED BLACK PEPPER
- 1/4 TSP RED PEPPER FLAKES CRUSHED
- 1/2 TSP HERB-SPICE MIX (PAPRIKA, CUMIN, CHILI POWDER)
- 1 EAR OF FRESH CORN ON THE COB
- 1 TBSP FRESH CHIVES
- 1/2 LEMON

18 MINUTES   2 SERVINGS

Instructions:

- Rub the chicken breast with 1 tbsp of olive oil, herb-spice combination, crushed black pepper, and smashed red pepper flakes. Place the seasoned side of the chicken on the hot area of the grill. put for 12 min on the grill

- Prepare the asparagus and lay it on the grill as the chicken is cooking. Sprinkle with black pepper and 2 tbsp of olive oil. Grill the asparagus for 5 to 7 min on each side.

- Half the ear of corn and brush with 1 tsp olive oil. Grill the corn for 3–4 mins, or until lightly roasted. Give a squeeze of lemon juice and the chopped chives when the corn has finished grilling.

- Toss chicken and asparagus with lemon juice to taste.

Suggestions:

- Salt can be replaced with fresh lemon juice and a dash of olive oil.

- When the asparagus begins to sear, move it to a portion of the grill that is not directly over the flame.

Nutritional Values: Calories 338kcal | Protein 30g | Fat 18g | Carbs 14g | Salt 58mg |Sugar 5g |Fibers 3.6g

Fajitas

INGREDIENTS

- 2 TBSP VEGETABLE OIL
- 1/2 LB. BEEF OR CHICKEN STRIPS
- 2 TBSP LIME OR LEMON JUICE
- 1 TSP CHILI POWDER
- 1/2 TSP CUMIN
- 1/4 GREEN OR RED PEPPER/SLICED LENGTHWISE
- 4 FLOUR TORTILLAS
- 1/2 TSP DRY CILANTRO

10 MINUTES   2 SERVINGS

Instructions:

- Heat the oven to 300°f.

- Heat vegetable oil in a nonstick frying pan over medium heat.

- Add the meat, spices, and lemon/lime juice; sauté for 5-10 min, or until the meat is cooked through

- Cook for 1-2 min after adding the peppers and onion to the pan.

- Take off the heat and stir in the cilantro.

- Place the tortillas on a baking sheet lined with foil and bake for 10 mins in the oven

- Distribute the mixture among the tortillas, wrap, and serve.

Nutritional Values Calories 184kcals | Protein 21g | Fat 6g | Carbs 20g | Salt 342mg | Sugar 3g | Fibers 5g

Chicken Stir-Fry with Snow Peas & Bell Pepper

INGREDIENTS

- 1/4 CUP OF LOW SODIUM CHICKEN BROTH
- 1 TBSP RICE VINEGAR
- 1/4 TBSP LOW SODIUM SOY SAUCE
- 1/2 TSP GRATED FRESH GINGER
- 1 MINCED CLOVE GARLIC
- 1/8 TSP BLACK PEPPER
- NONSTICK COOKING SPRAY
- 1 CUP OF FROZEN OR FRESH SNOW PEAS (THAWED IF FROZEN OR TRIMMED IF FRESH
- 1/8 CUP OF CHOPPED GREEN ONIONS
- 1 BELL PEPPER CHOPPED
- 1 TSP CANOLA OR CORN OIL
- 1/2 LBS. CHICKEN BREASTS SKINLESS BONELESS, (CUT INTO BITE-SIZE PIECES
- 1 TSP CORN STARCH
- 1/8 CUP OF WATER

12 MINUTES 2 SERVINGS

Instructions:

- Stir the broth, vinegar, soy sauce, ginger root, garlic, and pepper in a small bowl. Place aside.

- Coat a big skillet or wok with cooking spray. Cook the snow peas, green onions, and bell peppers for 4 to 5 minutes, or until tender but crisp, stirring periodically, over medium-high heat. Place on a platter.

- Warm the oil in the same pan, turning it around to cover the bottom. Fry the chicken for 4–5 minutes, stirring regularly until it is no longer pink in the center.

- Put the snow pea mixture back in the skillet. Incorporate the broth mixture. Still, over medium-high heat, bring to a boil. Cook for 1 minute, stirring now and then.

- In a small dish, combine the cornstarch and the water. Stir in the water to dissolve the cornstarch. Combine with the chicken mixture. Cook, stirring periodically, for 45 sec to 1 minute, or until thickened.

Nutritional Values: Calories 200kcal | Protein 27g | Fat 5g | Carbs 10g | Salt 290mg |Sugar 5g |Fibers 2g

Herb-Rubbed Pork Tenderloin

INGREDIENTS

- 1/4 TSP DRIED ROSEMARY
- 1/4 TSP DRIED THYME
- 1/4 TSP DRIED PARSLEY
- 1/2 TSP BLACK PEPPER
- 1/2 CLOVE GARLIC (FINELY MINCED)
- 1/2 TBSP DIJON MUSTARD
- 6 OZ PORK TENDERLOIN
- 1/2 TBSP VEGETABLE OIL

25 MINUTES   2 SERVINGS

Instructions:

- Combine rosemary, thyme, basil, parsley, and black pepper in a shallow dish. Mix in the mustard and garlic. Rub the herb mixture evenly over the pork tenderloins. Refrigerate the tenderloins for at least two hours, covered in plastic wrap.

- Preheat the oven to 400 degrees Fahrenheit.

- In a frying pan over med-heat, heat the oil. Brown the tenderloins from all sides in the oil. Take out from the skillet and arrange on a baking dish with plenty of room between them, so they do not touch.

- Bake for 20 min, or until a meat thermometer registers 165° F (rare)) to 175° F (medium to well done).

- Enable the tenderloins to stand for 10 to 15 min before cutting to allow the fluids to penetrate the flesh.

Nutritional Values: Calories 165kcal | Protein 24g | Fat 7g | Carbs 1g | Salt 140mg |Sugar 0g |Fibers 0g

Beef Stroganoff

INGREDIENTS

- 1/4 LBS. BEEF TENDERLOIN (SLICED INTO 2-INCH STRIPS)
- 2 OZ (UNCOOKED) WHOLE GRAIN EGG NOODLES
- 1/2 TSP OLIVE OIL
- 1/8 CUP ONION (MINCED)
- 1/2 TBSP ALL-PURPOSE FLOUR
- 1/4 CUP OF DRY WHITE WINE
- 1/2 CUP OF WHITE(BUTTON) MUSHROOMS (SLICED)
- 1/4 TSP DIJON MUSTARD
- 1/8 CUP OF SOUR CREAM FAT-FREE
- 1/4 CAN (14.5-OZ) LOW SODIUM BEEF BROTH FAT-FREE,
- A PINCH OF SALT(OPTIONAL)
- A PINCH OF BLACK PEPPER

30 MINUTES   2 SERVINGS

Instruction:

- Cook the noodles according to the package directions, omitting the salt.

- In a large frying pan over high heat, heat the oil. Sauté the meat for around 3 min. Remove the meat from the pan. Sauté the mushrooms and onion for 5 minutes, or until they brown.

- Cook for a minute after adding the flour. Cook for 2 min after adding wine to deglaze pan. Bring the Dijon mustard and beef stock to a boil. Lower the heat and continue to cook for 5 min.

- Return the steak and any juices to the broth and cook for 3 minutes. Simmer for 30 sec after adding sour cream, salt (optional), and pepper.

- Serve with whole-wheat egg noodles.

Nutritional Values: Calories 275kcal | Protein 23g | Fat 7g | Carbs 29g | Salt 250mg |Sugar 3g |Fibers 4g

Slow-Cooked Lemon Chicken

INGREDIENTS

- 1/2 TSP DRIED OREGANO
- 1/8 TSP GROUND BLACK PEPPER
- 1 TBSP BUTTER, UNSALTED
- 1/2-POUND CHICKEN BREAST, BONELESS, SKINLESS
- 1/8 CUP CHICKEN BROTH, LOW SODIUM
- 1/8 CUP WATER
- 1/2 TBSP LEMON JUICE
- 1 CLOVES GARLIC, MINCED
- 1/2 TSP FRESH BASIL, CHOPPED

180 MINUTES 2 SERVINGS

Instructions:

- In a mixing bowl, mix ground black pepper and oregano. Massage the mixture over the chicken.

- In a medium-sized pan over medium heat, melt the butter. Fry the chicken until brown in the melted butter before placing it in the slow cooker.

- Combine the water, chicken broth, garlic, and lemon juice in a pot. Bring it to a boil to release the browned pieces on the bottom of the skillet. Pour the sauce over the chicken.

- Cover and cook on high for 2 ½ hours or low for 5 hours.

- Baste the chicken after adding the basil. Cook for a further 15 to 30 min on high, or until the chicken is cooked.

Nutritional Values: Calories 197kcal | Protein 26g | Fat 9g | Carbs 1g | Salt 57mg |Sugar 2g |Fibers 0.3g

Jalapeño-Lime Turkey Burger with Smoked Mozzarella

INGREDIENTS

- 1/2 LB. GROUND TURKEY
- 1/2 TBSP JALAPEÑO, * FINELY DICED
- 1/4 TBSP FRESHLY GROUND BLACK PEPPER
- JUICE OF 1/2 LIMES AND ZEST** OF 1 LIME
- 1/4 TBSP WORCESTERSHIRE SAUCE, LOW SODIUM
- 1 TBSP EXTRA VIRGIN OLIVE OIL
- 2 HAMBURGER BUNS, TOASTED
- 2 SLICES OF MOZZARELLA CHEESE WITH SKIM MILK

20 MINUTES 2 SERVINGS

Instructions:

- In a medium-sized mixing bowl, combine the first 5 ingredients, plus 1/2 tbsp of olive oil. Make 4 equal-sized turkey burger patties and coat them gently with 1/2 tbsp of olive oil.

- Heat half of the canola oil in a large nonstick sauté pan over medium-high heat

- Fry the burgers for 5 to 7 minutes on each side, turning once or until a meat thermometer registers an internal temperature of 165° F.

- Melt the cheese on each burger in a toaster oven or a broiling oven.

- Each turkey burger should be served on a toasted bun add cheese to the burger. Let the cheese melt gently by leaving the grill open.

Nutritional Values: Calories 407kcal | Protein 32g | Fat 22g | Carbs 20g | Salt 435mg |Sugar 4g |Fibers 0.9g

Baked Salmon with Ginger-Citrus Sauce

INGREDIENTS

- 1 CUP OF ORANGE JUICE 50% REDUCED SUGAR
- 2 1/2-INCH- FRESH GINGER PIECE (PEELED & SLICED)
- 1/4 CUP OF SPLENDA GRANULATED SWEETENER
- 1/4 TSP CORN STARCH
- 2 TBSP FAT-FREE HALF-AND-HALF
- 2 TBSP LIGHT BUTTER WITH CANOLA
- 1/4 TSP SALT
- 8 OZ (4-OZ EACH) SALMON PORTIONS
- 2 CUP STIR-FRY VEGETABLES (FROZEN)

10 MINUTES   2 SERVINGS

Instructions:

- Heat oven to 450 degrees Fahrenheit.

- Make the sauce: Combine orange juice, sliced ginger and Splenda Sweetener in a saucepan. Bring the water to a boil over medium-high heat. Boil for 10–12 mins, or until the orange juice is reduced to 2 tbsp. Take off the heat and discard the ginger slices.

- In a mixing bowl, combine cornstarch, half-and-half, and salt until combined.

- A spoonful at a time, whisk butter into orange juice until it melts. Stir the half-and-half mixture in. Return the pot to medium-high heat and bring to a boil.

- Take off the sauce from the heat; move to a blender and process for 30 sec, or until light and creamy.

- Prepare the veggies and fish as follows: Arrange the veggies in a baking dish of 8"× 8" and top with the salmon fillets. Bake for 10 to 15 mins

- Transfer the veggies and fish to serving dishes; drizzle the sauce over the salmon. If preferred

Nutritional Values: Calories 290kcal | Protein 24g | Fat 15g | Carbs 16g | Salt 490mg |Sugar 8g |Fibers 2g

Bagel with Egg and Salmon

INGREDIENTS

- 1/2 BAGEL
- 1 LARGE EGG
- 1 TBSP CREAM CHEESE
- 1/2 TSP FRESH DILL
- 1 OZ COOKED SALMON
- 2 FRESH BASIL LEAVES
- 1 TBSP SCALLIONS
- 1 SLICE TOMATO
- 4 PIECES ARUGULA

2 MINUTES **2 SERVINGS**

Instructions:

- To toast one side of the bagel, cut it in half and bake it in the toaster or oven.
- Cut the dill, scallions, and basil leaves into small pieces. Blend in the cream cheese.
- Layer the cream cheese mixture over one-half of the toasted bagel, then top with arugula and a tomato slice.
- Scramble the egg in a frying pan sprayed with nonstick spray.
- While the egg is cooking, reheat the salmon in the same frying pan.
- Place the tomato slice on top of the egg and salmon. Enjoy!

Suggestions:

- Choose a 2-oz bagel for a reduced-carb sandwich.
- This is a terrific way to use up leftover salmon the next day.
- Fresh lettuce, spinach leaves, or micro-greens can be used in place of the arugula.

Nutritional Values: *Calories 318kcal | Protein 19g | Fat 14g | Carbs 29g | Salt 378mg |Sugar 3g |Fibers 2.6g*

Chilled Veggie & Shrimp Noodle Salad

INGREDIENTS

- 2 OZ DRY SPAGHETTI, NOODLES COOKED AND CHILLED (DON'T RINSE)
- 2-OZ PACK OF COOKED SALAD SHRIMP OR 1 CUP OF COCKTAIL SHRIMP, COOKED PEELED, DEVEINED, TAILLESS AND CUT IN HALF.
- 1/4 CUP FRESH CARROTS, SHREDDED
- 1 TBSP FRESH SCALLIONS, SLICED
- 1/4 CUPS FRESH SHITAKE MUSHROOMS, CHOPPED
- 1/4 CUPS FRESH BROCCOLI FLORETS
- 1/2 TSP CHILI OIL
- 2 TSP SESAME OIL
- 1 TBSP RICE WINE VINEGAR
- 1/2 TSP FRESH GINGER, CHOPPED
- 1 TBSP LOW-SODIUM SOY SAUCE SUBSTITUTE (RECIPE BELOW)
- 1 TSP FRESH GARLIC, CHOPPED
- 2 LIMES JUICED
- 1 LIME ZESTED

10 MINUTES   2 SERVINGS

Instructions:

- In a small saucepan, combine the ingredients for the soy sauce alternative.

- On medium heat, stirring constantly. Allow to reduce and thicken to around 1 cup. Refrigerate any leftovers.

- Then, combine the first 6 ingredients in a large mixing bowl and put them aside.

- In a blender, combine the other ingredients and mix for 1 minute or well combined.

- Pour the dressing over the spaghetti. Serve after tossing until evenly coated.

Nutritional Values: Calories 254kcal | Protein 13g | Fat 11g | Carbs 27g | Salt 433mg | Sugar 1g | Fibers 3g

Salmon Patties

INGREDIENTS

- 1 OZ (142 G) OF SOCKEYE SALMON, SKINLESS, BONELESS DRAINED AND RINSED
- 1/4 CUP OF WHITE ONION FINELY DICED
- 1/2 LARGE EGG, SLIGHTLY BEATEN
- 1/4 CUP OF BREADCRUMBS
- 1/4 CUP OF RED BELL PEPPER FINELY DICED
- 1/2 TBSP LEMON JUICE
- 1/4 TSP ROSEMARY, DRY CRUSHED
- 1/2 TSP LEMON PEEL GRATED
- PINCH OF GROUND PEPPER
- 1 TBSP VEGETABLE OIL

10 MINUTES 2 SERVINGS

Instructions:

- Put the salmon, egg, bell pepper, onion, breadcrumbs, lemon peel, rosemary, lemon juice, and black pepper in a mixing bowl and combine well.

- Shape the mixture into four patties. Refrigerate for about 30 min to allow it to solidify.

- Melt the butter in a large nonstick skillet over medium heat.

- Carefully place the patties in the pan and fry for 3–5 min each side, or until slightly browned.

- Serve the patties alone or with your favorite side, wrapped in lettuce or on a bun,

Nutritional Values: Calories 214kcal | Protein 17g | Fat 7g | Carbs 14g | Salt 373mg | Sugar 2g | Fibers 2g

Shrimp Tacos with Mango Salad

INGREDIENTS

SALSA:
- 1/3 RED BELL PEPPER MEDIUM, DICED
- 1 MANGOS, DICED
- 2 TBSP RED ONION, DICED
- 1 TBSP CHOPPED FRESH CILANTRO,
- 2 TBSP FRESH LIME JUICE
- 1/3 JALAPENO, DICED

TACO:
- 1/3 LB. SHRIMP, RAW DEVEINED AND PEELED
- 1 TSP FRESH LEMON JUICE
- A PINCH OF GROUND BLACK PEPPER
- 4 SOFT TACO SHELLS

20 MINUTES 2 SERVINGS

Instructions:

- Heat the oven to 350F.

- In a bowl, combine all of the mango salsa ingredients and chill until serving

- Coat the shrimp with lemon juice and season with black pepper in a baking dish.

- Bake the shrimp for 9- to 13 mins, or until they are pink and opaque.

- Fill taco shells with cooked shrimp and mango salsa.

Nutritional Values: Calories 320kcal | Protein 23g | Fat | Carbs 44g | Salt 562mg |Sugar 12g |Fibers 6g

Apple Crisp

INGREDIENTS

- 1 CUP OF RED APPLES (PEELED & SLICED)
- NONSTICK COOKING SPRAY
- 2 TBSP PACKED BROWN SUGAR
- 1/8 CUP OLD-FASHIONED ROLLED OATS (NOT QUICK COOKING)
- 2 TBSP ALL-PURPOSE FLOUR
- 2 TSP SOFTENED MARGARINE
- A PINCH OF GROUND CINNAMON
- A PINCH OF GROUND NUTMEG
- A PINCH OF VANILLA EXTRACT

20 MINUTES   2 SERVINGS

Instructions:

- Preheat the oven to 375 degrees Fahrenheit. Spray a baking dish of 13 x 9-inch with cooking spray.

- Put flour, brown sugar, oats, margarine, nutmeg, cinnamon, and vanilla in a small mixing dish. Using a fork, combine the ingredients until moistened (mixture should be crumbly).

- In a baking dish, layer the apples and generously sprinkle the brown sugar mixture on top. put 30 min in the oven to bake

Nutritional Values: *Calories 145kcal | Protein 2g | Fat 4g | Carbs 27g | Salt 40mg |Sugar |Fibers 2g*

Bagel Bread Pudding

INGREDIENTS

- 1/2 CUP OF ALMOND MILK
- 1 BAGEL MEDIUM-SIZED
- 1/4 CUP OF SUGAR
- 1 TSP CINNAMON
- 1/4 CUP OF EGG SUBSTITUTE LOW CHOLESTEROL

30 MINUTES   2 SERVINGS

Instructions:

- Heat the toaster or oven to 350 degrees Fahrenheit. Coat a small baking dish with nonstick cooking spray.
- Place the bagel in a baking dish and break it into tiny pieces.
- Combine egg product, cinnamon almond milk, and sugar in a mixing bowl, then pour over bagel pieces. Allow for a few mins for the bagels to absorb the liquid.
- Bake in the oven for 30 min, or until the top is golden. Serve chilled or hot. If desired, top with whipped topping.

Nutritional Values: Calories 222kcal | Protein 6g | Fat 2g | Carbs 45g | Salt 263mg |Sugar 14g |Fibers 1.7g

Sunburst Lemon Bars

INGREDIENTS

CRUST:
- 2 CUPS OF ALL-PURPOSE FLOUR
- 1/2 CUP OF POWDERED SUGAR
- 2 STICKS OR 1 CUP OF UNSALTED BUTTER, ROOM TEMPERATURE

FILLING:
- 1/4 CUP OF ALL-PURPOSE FLOUR
- 4 EGGS
- 1/2 TSP CREAM OF TARTAR
- 1 1/2 CUPS OF SUGAR
- 1/4 CUP LEMON JUICE
- 1/4 TSP BAKING SODA

GLAZE:
- 1 CUP OF SIFTED POWDERED SUGAR,
- 2 TBSP LEMON JUICE

25 MINUTES   2 SERVINGS

Instructions:

Crust:

- Heat the oven to 350 degrees Fahrenheit
- Mix the flour, 1 cup of softened butter and powdered sugar in a large mixing bowl. Combine until crumbly. Press the mixture into the bottom in a 9" x 13" baking pan.
- Bake for 15–20 min, or until gently browned.

Filling:

- Whisk the eggs lightly in a small bowl.
- In a separate bowl, stir together the flour, sugar, baking soda and cream of tartar,
- Combine the dry ingredients with the eggs. Whisk in the lemon juice until the egg mixture is significantly thickened.
- Layer over the heated crust and put in the oven for another 20 min; until the filling is set, layer over the heated crust.
- Take out from the oven and set aside to cool.

Glaze:

- Gently combine the sifted powdered sugar and lemon juice until smooth and creamy in a small mixing bowl. As required, adjust the amount of lemon juice.

- Spread the chilled filling on top. Allow the glaze to set before cutting into 24 bars. Refrigerate any leftover lemon bars.

Nutritional Values: Calories 200kcal | Protein 2g | Fat 9g | Carbs 28g | Salt 27mg |Sugar 11g |Fibers 0.3g

Cream Cheese Filled Strawberries

INGREDIENTS

- 4 STRAWBERRIES LARGE
- 2 TBSP CREAM CHEESE STRAWBERRY-FLAVORED
- 2 TSP SOUR CREAM REDUCED FAT
- 2 TBSP BLUEBERRIES (OPTIONAL)

10 MINUTES   2 SERVINGS

Instructions:

- Remove the tops of the strawberries and place them upright on the flat side.
- Make a thorough "x" in the top of each strawberry, taking care not to cut all the way through.
- Separate the berries gently.
- In a small mixing bowl, combine sour and cream cheese until smooth.
- The filling should be spooned or piped* into each strawberry.
- If desired, top with blueberries.
- Place in the refrigerator until ready to serve.

*If you *don't* have a piping bag, slit a corner of a zip-lock bag, and press the cream cheese filling into the strawberries.

Nutritional Values: Calories 56kcal | Protein 1g | Fat | Carbs 4g | Salt 30mg |Sugar5g |Fibers 8g

Blueberry Lemon Pound Cake

INGREDIENTS

- 3 EGGS
- 1/2 CUP OF COTTAGE CHEESE (NON-FAT)
- 2 TSP VANILLA EXTRACT
- 1/2 CUP OF BUTTER (UNSALTED, SOFTENED)
- 1 CUP OF NON-FAT LEMON YOGURT
- 1/4 CUP OF SPLENDA
- 1/2 CUP OF WHOLE WHEAT FLOUR
- 1 1/4 CUP OF ALL-PURPOSE FLOUR
- 1 TSP BAKING POWDER
- 2 TSP LEMON ZEST
- 1 CUP OF BLUEBERRIES
- 1/2 TSP BAKING SODA
- 1/2 TSP SALT

40 MINUTES 2 SERVINGS

Instructions:

- Heat the oven to 375°F.
- Puree the cottage cheese in a large mixing bowl until smooth.
- Blend butter, cottage cheese, and Splenda until smooth.
- Blend in the eggs, lemon juice, yogurt, lemon zest, and vanilla extract until creamy.
- Combine whole-wheat flour, all-purpose flour, salt, baking soda and baking powder into the mixing bowl.
- Blend the dry ingredients in a mixing bowl until smooth.
- Fold the blueberries into the pound cake batter gently.
- In a greased loaf pan that is 9" x 5", pour the batter.
- Bake for 35-40 min at 375°F.
- Allow cooling before serving

Nutritional Values: Calories 177kcal | Protein 5.4g | Fat 9.4g | Carbs 18.2g | Salt 203mg |Sugar 4g |Fibers 1.3g

Power Snack Mix

INGREDIENTS

- 1/4 CUP OF ALMONDS
- 1/2 CUP OF MULTIGRAIN CHEERIOS
- 1/8 CUP OF DRIED CHERRIES
- 1 TBSP MINI CHOCOLATE CHIPS

5 MINUTES   **2 SERVINGS**

Instructions:

- Mix all the ingredients in a medium mixing bowl. Divide into 1/3 cup portions.

- Enjoy 1 portion at a time

Nutritional Values: Calories 190kcal | Protein 4g | Fat 12g | Carbs 19g | Salt 20mg |Sugar 11g |Fibers 3g

Cucumber Sandwiches

INGREDIENTS

- 2 TBSP CREAM CHEESE
- 4 SLICES OF WHITE OR WHEAT BREAD
- 1/2 A CUCUMBER
- 1 TBSP MAYONNAISE
- 1/4 TSP DRY ITALIAN SALAD DRESSING MIX
- 1 PINCH OF DRIED DILL WEED

10 MINUTES 2 SERVINGS

Instructions:

- Get the cucumber, peeled, and sliced

- Combine the cream cheese, mayonnaise, and Italian dressing mix in a mixing bowl. Chill for at least one hour before serving.

- Spread the cream cheese mixture on white toast. Layer Cucumber slices on top and sprinkle dill.

- Sandwiches should be cut in half and served.

Nutritional Values: *Calories 253kcal | Protein 5g | Fat 13g | Carbs 29g | Salt 425mg |Sugar |Fibers 1.9g*

Sweet & Nutty Protein Bars

INGREDIENTS

- 2 1/2 CUPS OF ROLLED OATS, TOASTED
- 1/2 CUP OF ALMONDS
- 1/2 CUP OF FLAXSEEDS
- 1/2 CUP OF PEANUT BUTTER
- 1 CUP OF DRIED CHERRIES, BLUEBERRIES
- 1/2 CUP OF HONEY

10 MINUTES **2 SERVINGS**

Instructions:

- To toast the oats, place rolled oats on a baking tray and bake for ten minutes or lightly browned.

- Mix all of the ingredients until completely combined.

- Spread the protein mixture into a 9" × 9" pan that has been lightly oiled and pressed down tightly. Wrap in plastic wrap and place in the refrigerator for at least one hour or overnight.

- Serve protein bars cut into appropriate squares.

Nutritional Values: *Calories 283kcal | Protein 7g | Fat 13g | Carbs 39g | Salt 49mg |Sugar 2g |Fibers 5.8g*

Wheat Bran Muffins

INGREDIENTS

- 1/2 CUP OF WHITE SUGAR
- 1 EGG
- 1/2 CUP OF WHEAT BRAN
- 1 1/2 CUPS OF ALL-PURPOSE FLOUR
- 1/3 CUP OF VEGETABLE OIL
- 1 TSP VANILLA EXTRACT
- 1 1/2 TSP BAKING SODA
- 1 CUP OF UNFORTIFIED RICE BEVERAGE
- 1/2 CUP OF RASPBERRIES, FROZEN OR FRESH
- 1 CUP OF CRANBERRIES, FRESH OR FROZEN

20 MINUTES 12 SERVINGS

Instructions:

- Heat a standard oven to 350°F.

- Paper muffin cups should be used to line the muffin pans.

- In a large bowl, combine the sugar, egg, vanilla extract, and oil.

- Pour in the rice beverage and stir to blend.

- Mix the wheat bran, flour, and baking soda separately.

- Mix the dry ingredients completely with the wet components.

- Incorporate the berries into the muffin batter.

- Spoon the batter evenly among the 12 muffin cups and bake for about 20 min, or until the muffin tops spring back when touched.

Nutritional Values: Calories 181kcal | Protein 3g | Fat 7g | Carbs 26g | Salt 147mg |Sugar 10g |Fibers 2g

High Protein Energy Bites

INGREDIENTS

- 1/2 CUP OF UNSALTED PRETZELS CHOPPED
- 1 CUP OF CRISPY PUFFED RICE CEREAL
- 1/4 CUP OF HONEY
- 1/2 CUP OF PEANUT BUTTER
- 1/4 CUP OF DRIED CRANBERRIES
- 1/2 CUP OF CHOCOLATE CHIPS SEMISWEET
- 1/2 CUP OF ALMONDS, CHOPPED ROUGHLY
- 1 TBSP. OF CHIA SEEDS (OPTIONAL)
- 1/4 CUP OF GROUND FLAXSEED

10 MINUTES 25 SERVINGS

Instructions:

- In a large mixing bowl, combine all ingredients and stir until equally covered. Refrigerate for 1-2 hours, covered. (This will make it easier to handle the mixture.)

- Remove from the fridge and roll into 1-inch balls or press into the base of a baking paper to form granola bars.

- Refrigerate in a tightly covered jar for up to 2 weeks.

**It is not necessary to refrigerate these, although it helps the balls hold their form.

Nutritional Values: *Calories 118kcal | Protein 3.2g | Fat 7.3g | Carbs 12g | Salt 20mg |Sugar 11g |Fibers 2g*

Maple-Thyme Roasted Brussel Sprouts

INGREDIENTS

- 1/4 BUNCH OF FRESH THYME
- 1/2 LBS. FRESH BRUSSELS SPROUTS
- 1 CLOVE OF GARLIC MINCED
- 1 TSP MAPLE SYRUP
- 1/2 TBSP EXTRA-VIRGIN OLIVE OIL
- A PINCH OF BLACK PEPPER
- A PINCH SALT

25 MINUTES   2 SERVINGS

Instructions:

- Heat the oven to 450 degrees Fahrenheit.

- Snip and split Brussels sprouts in half; place in a medium mixing bowl. Pull the thyme leaves off the stalks and place them in the bowl.

- Toss together olive oil, garlic, maple syrup, pepper, and salt in a mixing bowl.

- Put out on a baking sheet in a uniform thickness. Put in the oven and bake for 20–25 min, or until the sprouts are tender to touch and beginning to brown.

Nutritional Values: Calories 80kcal | Protein 3g | Fat 4g | Carbs 11g | Salt 100mg |Sugar 3g |Fibers 3g

Crustless Asparagus and Tomato Quiche

INGREDIENTS

- 5 OZ ASPARAGUS 2-INCH PIECES
- 6 GRAPE OR CHERRY TOMATOES (CUT IN HALF)
- 2 GREEN ONIONS CHOPPED
- 1/2 CUP OF SKIM MILK
- 2 EGG WHITES
- 2 EGGS
- 1 TSP DIJON MUSTARD
- 1/4 TSP THYME DRIED, OR 1/2 TSP FRESH THYME CHOPPED
- 1/4 CUP OF LOW-FAT CHEDDAR CHEESE SHREDDED
- NONSTICK COOKING SPRAY
- 1/8 TSP BLACK PEPPER

40 MINUTES 2 SERVINGS

Instructions:

- Heat the oven to 350 degrees Fahrenheit. Coat cooking spray on a 9-inch glass pie pan lightly.

- Warm the oil in a medium nonstick pan over medium heat, turning to coat the base. Cook for 4 to 5 mins, or until the green onions and asparagus are tender. In the pie pan, layer the asparagus mixture and tomatoes.

- Mix the remaining ingredients, except the cheese, in a medium mixing dish. The mixture should be poured over the veggies. Garnish with cheese.

- Cook 30–35 min in the oven, or until a toothpick inserted in the middle comes out clean. Allow the quiche to cool slightly before dividing it into four equal pieces.

Nutritional Values: Calories 150kcal | Protein 15g | Fat 5g | Carbs 10g | Salt 280mg |Sugar 7g |Fibers 3g

Caraway Cabbage & Rice

INGREDIENTS

- 1/4 CUP OF WATER
- 1 CUP OF CABBAGE
- 1 TBSP WORCESTERSHIRE SAUCE
- 1 TBSP ONION
- 1/4 CUP OF CANNED MANDARIN ORANGES
- 1/2 TSP CARAWAY SEED
- 1 CUP OF RICE, COOKED
- NONSTICK COOKING SPRAY

15 MINUTES **2 SERVINGS**

Instructions:

- Chop the onion and shred the cabbage.
- Cook the onion and cabbage until soft in a nonstick frying pan sprayed with cooking spray.
- Pour in the water, Worcestershire sauce, and caraway seeds. Boil for 3 min. Stir often to prevent burning.
- Drain the mandarin oranges and add them to the cabbage mixture. Mix in the heated rice.
- Serve immediately after removing from the heat.

Nutritional Values: Calories 142kcal | Protein 3g | Fat 0g | Carbs 31g | Salt 101mg |Sugar 2g |Fibers 2.4g

Garden Vegetable Salad

INGREDIENTS

- 1/4 MEDIUM CUCUMBER
- 1 CUP OF LETTUCE
- 1/4 CUP OF BROCCOLI FLORETS
- 4 BABY CARROTS
- 1 TSP OLIVE OIL
- 2 TBSP BALSAMIC VINEGAR

10 MINUTES   2 SERVINGS

Instructions:

- All veggies should be cleaned, washed, and dried.

- Place lettuce in a salad dish and coarsely chop it.

- Place cucumber slices on top of lettuce.

- Place 4 baby carrots in a salad dish and chop or shred them.

- Broccoli florets should be cut or broken into bite-size pieces.

- Pour the balsamic vinegar and olive oil over the salad.

- Toss gently and serve.

Suggestions:

A low-sodium Italian dressing or another favorite salad dressing might be used in place of olive oil and balsamic vinegar.

To enhance the protein intake, a cooked chicken breast can be added.

Nutritional Values: *Calories 98kcal | Protein 1g | Fat 5g | Carbs 10g | Salt 50mg |Sugar 1g |Fibers 2g*

Black Bean Burger & Cilantro Slaw

INGREDIENTS

- 1/4 CUP BLACK BEANS RINSED, DRAINED, DRIED AND MASHED (LOW SODIUM)
- 1/4 CUP BULGUR WHEAT (TO PREPARE MIX 1/2 CUP OF BULGUR WHEAT WITH ½ CUP OF HOT WATER AND LET SIT FOR 30 MIN)
- 1/4 TSP GROUND BLACK PEPPER
- 1/8 TSP SMOKED PAPRIKA
- 1/4 TSP GRANULATED GARLIC
- 2 TBSP SCALLIONS
- 1 TSP WORCESTERSHIRE SAUCE, LO SODIUM
- 1 TSP BEEF BOUILLON, LO SODIUM
- 1/8 TSP ONION FLAKES
- 1/8 CUP ONIONS
- 1/2 TBSP FLOUR
- 1/2 TBSP CILANTRO
- 1 CUP OF SLAW MIX
- 1/2 TBSP CANOLA OIL FOR SEARING*
- 2 TBSP BALSAMIC VINEGAR
- 1/2 TBSP SESAME OIL
- ZEST OF ONE LIME
- 2 TBSP LIME JUICE
- 2 HAMBURGER ROLLS
- 2 TBSP MAYONNAISE

20 MINUTES 2 SERVINGS

Instructions:

- Preheat the oven to 400 degrees Fahrenheit.

- Combine bulgur wheat, black beans, granulated garlic, beef bouillon, crushed black pepper, Worcestershire sauce, smoked paprika, onion flakes, 1/2 cup of scallions and onions, in mixing bowl.

- Form approximately 1/2 cup of the mixture into burgers and place in the freezer or refrigerator

- Vinaigrette may be made by combining lime juice, 1 tbsp cilantro, vinegar, and sesame oil. Add all except 2 tbsp of vinaigrette to slaw mix in a small bowl, gently combine, and set away in the chill.

- Set aside the 2 tbsp vinaigrette and mayonnaise remaining in a separate small dish.

- Flour the black bean burgers and shake off any excess. Spritz the tops of the burgers and place them on a pre-sprayed pan. Bake for 14 min, flipping burgers halfway through.

- Toast the bread and spread them with equal quantities of mayo. Top with the black bean burger and 1/4 cup (or preferred quantity) of slaw.

- *Nutritional Values:* Calories 380kcal | Protein 9g | Fat 19g | Carbs 45g | Salt 520mg |Sugar 4g |Fibers 5g

Better Mashed Potatoes

INGREDIENTS

- 1/3 HEAD OF CAULIFLOWER (SMALL FLORETS)
- 1/4 CUP OF LOW-FAT BUTTERMILK
- 1/2 BAKING OR RUSSET POTATO (2-INCH CUBES)
- 1 CLOVE OF GARLIC
- 1 TSP OLIVE OIL
- 1/2 TBSP GRATED PARMESAN CHEESE
- 1/2 TSP BUTTER
- A PINCH SALT
- A PINCH OF BLACK PEPPER

20 MINUTES   2 SERVINGS

Instructions:

- Place the potato, cauliflower, and garlic, in a large saucepan with enough water to cover it. Bring to a boil, then reduce to medium heat and simmer for 15 min, or until the potato and cauliflower are cooked.

- Return the veggies and garlic to the pot after draining. Cover the saucepan with a kitchen towel and place the lid on top. Allow for a 5-minute resting period. Take off the lid and the cloth. This procedure aids in the drying of the veggies, allowing them to mash more easily.

- Combine the olive oil, buttermilk, salt, cheese, butter, and pepper in a mixing bowl. *Mash* the ingredients until they are gently blended. Garnish with fresh chopped chives if desired.

Nutritional Values: Calories 60kcal | Protein 2g | Fat 2g | Carbs 7g | Salt 230mg |Sugar 2g |Fibers 2g

Armando's Chiles Rellenos

INGREDIENTS

- **4 OZ CREAM CHEESE**
- **1/4 CUP OF FRESH MUSHROOMS, SLICED**
- **1 TSP ONION**
- **1 TBSP CARROT**
- **1 EGG WHITE**
- **2 CALIFORNIA GREEN CHILI PEPPERS**
- **1 CUP OF CANOLA OIL**
- **1 TSP ALL-PURPOSE WHITE FLOUR**

10 MINUTES   2 SERVINGS

Instructions:

- Carrot and onion should be minced.

- Mix cream cheese, mushrooms, carrot, and onion to create stuffing in a mixing bowl. Set aside in the refrigerator until the chili peppers are ready.

- Melt butter in a frying pan over medium heat. Roast the peppers in a pan, tossing them several times until the skin bubbles. Turn off the heat. Take the skin off the peppers when they are cool enough to handle.

- Cut the chili peppers half lengthwise and scoop half of the cream cheese filling inside each pepper.

- In another dish, whisk together the egg white and flour until stiff. Brush the egg mixture over each filled chili pepper.

- Pour enough canola oil into a saucepan to cover the bottom by about an inch. Warm over medium-high heat.

- Place the chili peppers carefully in the heated oil and cook until golden brown, rotating once. Serve immediately.

Suggestions:

- Anaheim chili peppers, also known as California green chili peppers, are long green peppers with a pleasantly fiery flavor. If fresh green chili peppers are not available, use low sodium canned whole green chili peppers.
- The potassium concentration of chili peppers varies, with some types carrying more than 300 mg potassium per serving. Before using different types of chili peppers in this dish, consult with your dietician.

Nutritional Values: *Calories 304kcal | Protein 7g | Fat 28g | Carbs 6g | Salt 259mg |Sugar 1g |Fibers 1.3g*

Creamy Cucumber Salad

INGREDIENTS

- 1/3 CUP OF SOUR CREAM
- 1 MEDIUM CUCUMBER
- 2 TBSP WHITE VINEGAR
- 1/8 TSP BLACK PEPPER
- 1 TBSP SUGAR
- 1 TBSP FRESH DILL WEED

6 MINUTES   2 SERVINGS

Instructions:

- Cucumber should be thinly sliced.
- Sour cream, pepper sugar (or sweetener), and vinegar in a mixing bowl.
- Cucumbers should be added to the mixture. Before serving, chill the dish.
- If desired, garnish with fresh chopped dill weed.

Suggestions:

- Add 2 tbsp minced onion or chives for a different flavor.
- Use fat-free sour cream instead of normal sour cream for a lighter version.
- If you like, lemon juice can be used instead of vinegar.

Nutritional Values: Calories 94kcal | Protein 1g | Fat 6g | Carbs 9g | Salt 26mg |Sugar 2g |Fibers 0.5g

Mashed Carrots & Ginger

INGREDIENTS

- 1 1/2 CUPS OF BABY CARROTS
- 1/4 TSP FRESH GINGER, CHOPPED
- 1/4 TSP HONEY
- 1/4 TSP BLACK PEPPER
- 1/4 TSP VANILLA EXTRACT
- OPTIONAL GARNISH: FRESH CHIVES, CHOPPED

10 MINUTES 2 SERVINGS

Instructions:

- Carrots should be steamed or boiled on high heat until extremely soft. Reduce to low heat and mash carrots with a potato masher.
- Stir in the other ingredients (ginger, vanilla essence pepper, and honey) until completely combined.
- Sprinkle with chopped chives before serving.

Nutritional Values: Calories 30kcal | Protein | Fat 0g | Carbs 7g | Salt 55mg | Sugar 4g | Fibers 2g

Cauliflower Steak

INGREDIENTS

- 1/2 A HEAD OF CAULIFLOWER, SMALL TO MEDIUM SIZE
- 2 TBSP OIL AVOCADO OR CANOLA OR OLIVE OIL
- 1 CLOVES GARLIC, MINCED
- 1/2 TSP GARAM MASALA
- 1/3 TSP TURMERIC
- 1/4 TSP CUMIN
- PINCH OF SALT AND PEPPER

20 MINUTES   2 SERVINGS

Instructions:

- Heat the oven to 450 degrees Fahrenheit. Combine the oil, cumin, garam masala, garlic, and turmeric in a small mixing bowl. Season with pepper and salt.

- Place the cauliflower stem side up on a firm surface. Split the cauliflower in half vertically across the stem (the stem will help to keep the steak intact).

- Beginning on the flat side of each half, measure in 1 inch and slice down vertically to create a 1-inch thick "steak."

- Over medium heat, heat a big, heavy oven-proof skillet. Drizzle spicy oil over cauliflower and massage

- Cook for 8–10 minutes, or until the bottom side is nutty brown but not burned.

- Transfer the steaks and leftover cauliflower florets to a baking sheet lined with parchment paper. Bake for 15 min, or until the cauliflower is soft all the way through and the bottom is golden.

- If desired, remove the cauliflower from the oven and serve plain or with a yogurt drizzle.

Nutritional Values: Calories 87kcal | Protein 1.6g | Fat 2g | Carbs 4.4g | Salt 41mg |Sugar 2g |Fibers 6g

Chilled Persian Cucumber Soup with Chives

INGREDIENTS

- 3/4 CUP OF GREEK YOGURT (PLAIN FAT-FREE)
- 1 ENGLISH OR PERSIAN CUCUMBER (UNPEELED & GRATED COARSELY)
- FRESH CHIVES
- 1 TSP MINCED SHALLOTS
- 1 TSP FRESH MINT LEAVES CHOPPED FINELY
- 1/2 TSP MINCED GARLIC CLOVE
- 1/4 TSP FRESHLY GROUND BLACK PEPPER, OR TO TASTE
- 1/2 TBSP WHITE BALSAMIC OR CHAMPAGNE VINEGAR
- A PINCH OF SEA SALT, OR TO TASTE
- 1/4 CUP UNSWEETENED CHILLED JASMINE OR GREEN TEA (MADE WITH 1 TEA BAG)

30 MINUTES 2 SERVINGS

Instructions:

- In a medium mixing bowl, combine the yogurt, cucumber, mint, 2 tbsp of chives, garlic, shallot, vinegar, salt, tea, and pepper. Season to taste. Refrigerate until ready to be served.

- Divide the soup amongst small soup cups or bowls. Serve with the remaining 1 tsp chives on top.

Nutritional Values: Calories 140kcal | Protein 13g | Fat 4.5g | Carbs 14g | Salt 410mg | Sugar 5g | Fibers 1g

Asian Soup Jar

INGREDIENTS

- 1/2 CUP OF FROZEN CAULIFLOWER BROCCOLI, AND CARROTS
- 1 TBSP SHREDDED CARROT
- 1/2 CUP OF COOKED BROWN OR WHITE RICE
- 1/2 CUP OF SHREDDED CABBAGE
- 1 TSP SESAME OIL
- 1/2 TSP FRESH GRATED GINGER
- 1 TSP COCONUT AMINOS
- 1/2 TSP GARLIC POWDER
- 1 HARD COOKED EGG
- CRUSHED RED PEPPER FLAKES TO TASTE (OPTIONAL)

20 MINUTES   2 SERVINGS

Instructions:

- Boil the egg in a pot of water

- Turn off the heat and let the egg in the water for 8 min. Drain the water and replace it with cold water to chill the egg.

- In a 16 oz. Glass jar, layer rice and veggies.

- Combine coconut aminos, sesame oil, ginger, garlic powder, and red pepper flakes in a small mixing bowl. Serve with rice and veggies. Refrigerate after covering with a lid.

- Take out the jar from the refrigerator at least 15 - 20 before serving.

- Fill the jar with 5 oz of hot water, seal the top, and shake to blend. Allow ingredients to soak for 2 min in an unopened container.

- The hard-boiled egg should be peeled and sliced. Pour the contents of the jar into a dish, top with an egg, and serve!

Nutritional Values: Calories 267kcal | Protein 10g | Fat 11g | Carbs 32g | Salt 187mg |Sugar 2g |Fibers 4.6g

Chicken Rice Soup

INGREDIENTS

- 1/4 CUP OF LONG GRAIN WHITE RICE, UNCOOKED
- 1/4 CUP OF CARROTS, CHOPPED
- 1/4 TBSP ONION, MINCED
- 1/ 2 (ABOUT 2 OZ) CHICKEN BREASTS COOKED
- 1/4 TBSP FRESH PARSLEY, MINCED
- 2 TBSP ALL-PURPOSE WHITE FLOUR
- 1 TSP BUTTE
- 2 CUPS OF CHICKEN BROTH LOW SODIUM

10 MINUTES   2 SERVINGS

Instructions:

- Mix rice, 2 cups of chicken broth, and half a cup of water in a mixing bowl. Cook in a rice cooker or a stovetop

- In a saucepan, melt the butter. Sauté the onion until it is soft.

- Mix in the flour. Add the remaining chicken in batches.

- Cook, stirring regularly, over medium heat until the mixture thickens.

- Mix in the chicken, rice, and carrots. Simmer for 5 min.

- Before serving, garnish with parsley.

*For patients on a low potassium diet, the carrots should be cooked separately, and the water removed before being added to the soup.

Nutritional Values: Calories 220kcal | Protein 10g | Fat 7g | Carbs 23g | Salt 153mg |Sugar 3g |Fibers 4g

63

Kidney-Friendly Mushroom Soup

INGREDIENTS

- 1 TBSP COCONUT OIL
- A PINCH OF FRESH GROUND BLACK PEPPER
- 1/2 STALKS CELERY, CHOPPED
- 1 MEDIUM SHALLOT, FINELY DICED
- 4-OZ BUTTON OR CREMINI MUSHROOMS, SLICED
- 1/2 CLOVE GARLIC, FINELY DICED
- 1 TBSP FLOUR
- 1 SMALL BAY LEAVES
- 1 1/2 CUPS OF LOW SODIUM VEGETABLE STOCK, DIVIDED
- 1 SPRIG OF FRESH THYME
- 2 TBSP REGULAR YOGURT OR NON-DAIRY YOGURT

20 MINUTES   2 SERVINGS

Instructions:

- Begin by heating coconut oil in a big Dutch oven or saucepan for your kidney-friendly mushroom soup.

- Stir in the ground pepper, shallots, and celery. Cook on medium-high heat.

- Cook for 2 mins, stirring regularly until browned and aromatic.

- Turn the heat down to medium. Cook for 2 min more after adding the garlic.

- Mix in the cut mushrooms. Let the mushrooms release all their liquid by sautéing for 10 minutes, stirring regularly.

- Over the sautéed items, sprinkle the flour. Mix and toast for 1 or-2 min on medium heat.

- Add a cup of hot stock, bay leaves and thyme sprigs to the pot. Add the second cup of stock to the mushroom soup and stir to combine. To properly blend, stir everything together.

- Combine the remaining two cups of stock l. Cook for 15 min, or until the mushroom soup thickens.

- Pick out the bay leaves and thyme sprigs.

- In the saucepan, use an immersion blender or transfer the liquid to a blender.

- Puree the ingredients until it is as smooth as it can be.

- If using a blender, return the mushroom soup to the saucepan. Blend in the yogurt until smooth.

- Return to heat and simmer for 4 min more.

- Serve the kidney-friendly mushroom soup garnished with herbs or mushroom slices.

Nutritional Values: *Calories 127kcal | Protein 3g | Fat 8g | Carbs 13g | Salt 109mg |Sugar 2g |Fibers 2g*

Curried Carrot Soup

INGREDIENTS

- 1/3 MEDIUM ONION, DICED
- 1 TBSP AVOCADO OIL
- 2 CUPS OF BABY CARROTS
- 1/2 TBSP CURRY POWDER
- 1 1/2 TBSP OF FRESH GINGER, CHOPPED FINELY
- 1/8 TSP RED PEPPER FLAKES, TO TASTE
- 1 CAN (5 OZ) OF COCONUT MILK, RESERVE 2 TBSP FOR GARNISH
- 1 CUP OF LOW SODIUM VEGETABLE BROTH
- A DASH OF SEA SALT, TO TASTE
- A PINCH OF BLACK PEPPER, TO TASTE

GARNISH:
- 2 TBSP OF RESERVED COCONUT MILK
- 1 TBSP CHIVES, FINELY CHOPPED
- OPTIONAL: A SQUEEZE OF LEMON JUICE TO TASTE

30 MINUTES   2 SERVINGS

Instructions:

- Heat avocado oil in a saucepan over medium heat. Then add the chopped onion and simmer for 5-10 min, or until soft and aromatic.

- Cook for 5 min more, then add the or until the ginger is aromatic and baby carrots are tender.

- Stir in the curry powder and red pepper flakes for 30 to 60 sec, or until aromatic. Take care not to overcook the spices.

- When the spices are aromatic, add the vegetable broth and most coconut milk, saving 1/4 cup for garnish. Bring to a mild boil, then reduce to low heat, cover, and leave to simmer for 15-10 min

- Once the carrots are cooked, carefully mix the soup with an immersion blender until smooth and creamy. Alternatively, allow the soup to cool somewhat before blending it in stages using a strong blender. Season with salt and pepper to taste.

- To serve, sprinkle with conserved coconut milk, finely chopped chives

Nutritional Values: Calories 286kcal | Protein 3g | Fat 25g | Carbs 15.9g | Salt 256.1mg |Sugar 4g |Fibers 4.4g

Fruit and Almond Smoothie

INGREDIENTS

- 1/2 CUP OF GREEK YOGURT PLAIN NONFAT
- 1 CUP OF ALMOND MILK UNSWEETENED
- 1 CUP OF FROZEN KIWI

5 MINUTES   2 SERVINGS

Instructions:

- Put all ingredients into the blender and blend until smooth and thick.

Nutritional Values: Calories 100kcal | Protein 5g | Fat 2.5g | Carbs 15g | Salt 110mg |Sugar 4g |Fibers 2g

4 WEEK MEAL PLAN

WEEK	BREAKFAST	LUNCH	SNACK	DINNER
1 WEEK	Apple Crisp	Chicken Stir-Fry with Snow Peas & Bell Pepper	Armando's Chiles Rellenos	Cauliflower Steak
2 WEEK	Wheat Bran Muffins	Jalapeño-Lime Turkey Burger with Smoked Mozzarella	Cucumber Sandwiches	Black Bean Burger & Cilantro Slaw
3 WEEK	Avocado Toast with Egg	BBQ Chicken Pita Pizza	Apple Crisp	Creamy Cucumber Sala
4 WEEK	Fajitas	Herb-Rubbed Pork Tenderloin	Fruit and Almond Smoothie	Beef Stroganoff

Conclusion

Eating a balanced diet is critical for maintaining health with CKD (chronic kidney disease).

One may need to alter their diet in order to manage chronic renal disease (CKD). Consult a qualified dietitian to establish a meal plan that incorporates foods you love while also promoting kidney health.

The instructions below will assist you in eating healthfully while managing your renal condition. The first three phases (1-3) are critical for everyone suffering from renal disease. The latter two phases (4-5) may become more critical if your kidney function deteriorates.

1: Select and prepare foods that are low in salt and sodium

What for? To assist in the regulation of your blood pressure. Your diet should contain no more than 2,300 mg of salt each day.

Always purchase fresh food. Sodium (a component of salt) is added to many prepared or packaged meals sold in supermarkets and restaurants.

Prepare foods from scratch rather than relying on prepared foods, "fast" foods, frozen dinners, and canned foods containing high salt content. When you create your own meals, you have complete control over the ingredients.

Instead of salt, substitute spices, herbs, and sodium-free seasonings.

Verify the sodium content of food products using the Nutrition Facts label. The sodium content of 20% or higher of the Daily Value indicates that the food is rich in sodium.

Consider low-sodium frozen meals and other convenience items.

Before consuming canned vegetables, beans, meats, and fish, thoroughly rinse them with water.

Look for salt-free or sodium-free on food labels, no salt or reduced, low, sodium on food labels, or lightly salted or unsalted.

A Nutrition Facts label illustrates a 5% daily salt value per serving.

Check the salt content on food labels. A food label with a Percent Daily Value of 5% or less is considered low sodium. Additionally, check the label for the amount of saturated and trans fats.

2: Consume the appropriate amount and kind of protein

What for? To aid in the protection of your kidneys. Whenever your body utilizes protein, waste is produced. Your kidneys are responsible for removing this waste. Consuming more protein than necessary might cause your kidneys to work harder.

Consume minimal amounts of protein-rich meals.

Protein is present in both plant and animal-based meals. The majority of individuals consume both forms of protein. Consult your dietician for assistance in determining the optimal protein mix for you.

Foods containing animal protein:

- Dairy
- Meat

- Fish
- Chicken
- Eggs

A cooked chunk of chicken, fish, or beef weighs around 2 to 3 ounces and is roughly the size of a deck of cards. 12 cup milk or yogurt, or one slice of cheese is a portion of dairy foods.

Plant-based protein sources:

- Nuts
- Beans
- Grains

A portion of cooked beans is around ½ a cup, whereas a serving of nuts is approximately 1/4 cup. A piece of bread is considered a portion, but a cup of cooked rice or noodles is considered a portion.

3: Consume heart-healthy foods

What for? To assist in preventing fat accumulation in your blood vessels, heart, and kidneys.

Reduce your intake of saturated and trans fats. Consult the food label.

Instead of butter, use nonstick cooking spray or a little quantity of olive oil.

Instead of deep-frying dishes, grill, bake, broil, stir or -fry roast them.

Before eating, trim fat from meat and skin from chicken.

Foods that are beneficial to the heart:

- Fruits
- Cuts of beef that are lean, such as loin or round
- Beans
- Skinless poultry
- Fish
- Vegetables
- Milk, yogurt, and cheese that are low in fat or fat-free

Consume heart-healthy meals to assist in protecting your blood vessels, heart, and kidneys.

Consume alcohol in moderation: no more than one drink per day for women and two drinks per day for men. Consuming an excessive amount of alcohol may have a detrimental effect on the liver, heart, and brain, resulting in major health concerns. Consult your health care practitioner to determine the maximum amount of alcohol you may consume safely.

The following measures toward a healthy diet

As kidney function declines, patients may need to consume less phosphorus and potassium-containing foods. Your health care worker will do laboratory testing to determine your blood, phosphorus, and potassium levels, and you can work with your nutritionist to adapt your food plan. Nutrition for Advanced Chronic Kidney Disease is an NIDDK health topic that contains further information.

4: Consume meals and beverages that are low in phosphorus

What for? To assist in the protection of your blood vessels and bones. When you have CKD (chronic kidney disease), phosphorus can accumulate in your blood. Too much phosphorus in the blood draws calcium from the bones, causing them to become thin, weak, and more prone to fracture. Additionally, elevated phosphorus levels in the blood can cause itchy skin and bone and joint discomfort.

Numerous packaged foods include phosphorus. On ingredient labels, look for phosphorus—or terms beginning with "PHOS."

Phosphorus may be added to deli meats and certain fresh fowl and beef. Solicit assistance from the butcher in selecting fresh foods free of added phosphorus.

The health care physician may suggest that you take a phosphate binder with food to help reduce your blood phosphorus level. A phosphate binder is a medication that operates similarly to a sponge, absorbing or binding phosphorus in the stomach. Because the phosphorous is bonded, it does not enter the bloodstream. Rather than that, your body eliminates phosphorous via your feces.

5: Consume meals that have an adequate level of potassium

What for? To assist your muscles and nerves in functioning properly. When blood potassium levels are either too low or too high, complications might ensue. Damaged kidneys increase potassium levels in the blood, which can cause major cardiac issues. If necessary, your diet and beverage choices might assist you in lowering your potassium level.

Potassium levels in salt replacements may be rather high. Examine the ingredient list. Consult your provider on the use of salt alternatives.

Before consuming canned veggies and fruits, drain them.

Certain medications may also cause an increase in your potassium level. Your health care physician may need to alter the medications you are already taking.

Printed in Great Britain
by Amazon

26069403R00044